TALK BACK TO ME

A Radical Guide to Growing Up

 ONE IDEA PRESS

Ordering Information:
Quantity sales. Special discounts are available on quantity purchases by corporations, associations, and others. For details, contact the "Special Sales Department" at the following email address: hello@oneideapress.com.

Paperback: 978-1-944134-54-9
Hardcover: 978-1-944134-55-6

Printed in the United States of America

For Aiden and Ember

CONTENTS

BEFORE WE BEGIN

We parents love to tell you to think critically, don't believe everything you hear, and stand up for what you believe. We also want you to just shut up and to do things our way. We are a living paradox, and in turn we're giving you mixed messages and wildly inconsistent responses. You are likely to point this out, and we are likely to sigh and change the subject.

It's been nearly impossible to write this because as soon as I think I've finished a section, I'll have a new insight and want to add to it, change it, or rewrite it all together. I could be revising this book until I'm on my deathbed, typing with arthritic hands in between bites of pureed potatoes, and it would still be incomplete, imperfect, and deeply flawed. That's how growth works. It never stands still. So what you're getting here is a snapshot from one moment in time. That's all we ever really have, and it's the perfect place to start.

I'll do my best to share principles that will help you get what you want out of life, and I'll leave the details up to you. Weigh what you read here with your own internal sense of what's right. Because underneath it all I have a tremendous faith in who you are: good hearted, loving, passionate—and a little too smart for your own good.

BASIC TRAINING

If you were to ask my advice on just about any topic, you'd get it along with an unsolicited check-in about basic self care. That's why we're starting here. The rest of this book is dedicated to helping you get what you want out of life, and in order to do that you'll need energy and a clear head.

Any time you feel "off," whether you're dragging through your days, having a hard time concentrating, or feeling edgy and emotional, always come back to these three things. They're the foundation you need to pull yourself up, manage your own headspace, and take the right action.

Nutrition: I'm not telling you anything you don't already know, so I'll be brief: less sugar, fewer processed foods, more protein, and more veggies. Or as my doctor says, "Eat things that will rot." Pair that with a good water intake and you're golden.

Sleep: I know teens are naturally nocturnal, so I'm not going to prescribe my old-lady bedtime schedule for you. But if you're waking up still feeling tired, you're either not sleeping enough, or you're not sleeping well enough. If you're getting in the recommended 8-10 hours and still wake up feeling like you've been hit by a bus, then try getting off screens for a couple of hours before bed. You'll feel restless and edgy, but hang in there. It gets easier. It's good to rediscover that it is indeed possible to calm your mind and body without your phone next to your face whispering sweet nothings until you drift off to sleep.

Activity: This is a sneaky one, because lack of activity turns into a total and complete resistance to it. When you sit around the house day after day, even the idea of walking around the block sounds so *UGH*, let alone a bike ride or, heaven forbid, trudging up a mountain. This is one where you have to just decide that your feelings about it are irrelevant and force yourself to do it because it's good for you. It'll only take a few times of forcing it before you'll start to feel the resistance get lighter, and one magnificent day you might even crave it. But this is an area where you can't wait for motivation. Motivation will come only after you take an unmotivated action.

On the flip side, some of us have a tendency to become overactive when we're out of balance. I used to spend every workout class doing burpees until I could hardly stand while simultaneously calculating what it would take to feel good about my body: *Okay, if I do Pilates 3 times a week that takes care of core, then I'd need like 2 or 3 days of weight training, a couple of HIIT classes for functional fitness, and then maybe 3 rowing*

10

classes a week for cardio. Oh and then 3 or 4 days of yoga to stay flexible so I don't get injuries. Hmm...I could double up classes on Tuesdays, Thursdays, and Saturdays.... The thing I was supposedly doing for health was soooo unhealthy. And guess what? I burned out my adrenals to the point where I could hardly drag myself through any one of those activities, and when I did I'd be exhausted on the couch for 2 days. My doctor put me on a 6-month exercise restriction and it was almost a year before I could really exert myself and still feel good the next day. Compulsive exercise is like any other compulsion, but it's easy to disguise as a healthy habit. Don't fall into that trap.

If you feel really crappy, all three of these things are usually off at once. When this happens, it's a lot to ask of yourself to overhaul your entire life—and you won't have the energy to do that anyway. To drag yourself out of that quicksand, just pick one and take a small step toward it. I tend to start with nutrition, which usually means slowing down on chocolate and replacing it with something that has an actual nutrient or two, like a spinach smoothie. Boring, I know. But when my blood sugar is steady, I sleep better. And when I'm more rested, I feel more like exercising and don't feel so wiped out after a workout. A success in one area helps you get traction on all three, and you'll be surprised at how quickly you can pick yourself back up.

Once you've made any sort of tiny, wobbly progress in the three basics, there's one more thing to look at: stress. School stress may be the most obvious kind for you, but the one that can really get you is relationship stress. If you're having conflict with someone over a long period of time or constantly feeling on eggshells trying to *avoid* conflict, that stress is a slow energy leak. Over time, that leak will completely drain your reserves. We'll talk more about how to deal with people later. For now, just keep an eye on where your stress is happening so you can identify those energy leaks and start coming up with solutions to change your situation.

No matter what path you take as you grow up, you're going to need all of your energy to go all in on the things that matter most to you. Tending to the basics is the foundation for getting what you want in life and enjoying yourself along the way.

THE *YEAH BUT* MONSTER

Sometimes you'll want something that makes no sense. It feels frivolous, irrelevant, and out of reach. Sometimes it requires resources you don't have right this moment. But it keeps nagging at you. You find yourself daydreaming about it...and then right on the heels of the daydream comes the *Yeah But* Monster.

I want to go see Machu Picchu. *Yeah but with what money?*

I want to learn hip hop dance. *Yeah but I'm kind of old to start that now.*

I want to write a book. *Yeah but I don't have time.*

Right now I am obsessed with having a little backyard writing cottage, where early every morning I'll wander out in my pajamas and flip flops with a hot cup of coffee and sit at my beautiful wooden desk surrounded by succulents and ferns while the sun streams in through the upper window, and I'll write. I picture it in my head, and right on schedule, here's the *Yeah But* Monster. *Yeah but I'm just renting this house, I can't go putting a cottage back there. And with what money? Plants? When's the last time I kept a plant alive? A whole cottage just for me? Just for writing? I'm not even Oprah-level famous. Maybe I'm not even a real writer. What makes me think I deserve something like a cottage?*

See what I mean? The *Yeah But* Monster is SAVAGE.

And yet....Ohhhhhh how I want that cottage.

When the *Yeah But* Monster shows up, you know you're onto something good. He doesn't bother with the little stuff. Take note, and then pat the poor creature on the head and send him to bed. Because it doesn't matter if you don't have the details worked out, or if it feels so out of reach that you can't imagine how to get there. The point is, you want this thing. Let yourself want it. Let yourself feel the way it burns in your belly. Let it be uncomfortable.

This thing you want is sacred. It's calling to you. You don't have to know why—in fact, most of the time you CAN'T know why. Just know that it's beckoning to you for a reason, and it deserves your full attention. Maybe it's calling you to a particular destination, or maybe it's the first of many stepping stones down the path to something so fulfilling it'll take your breath away. Let it be there. Let it not make sense.

Next, you're probably expecting me to tell you to make a list of what you need to do to get there. What are your steps?

What are your goals and sub-goals and sub-sub-goals with checklists and action steps and sticky notes and due dates and accountability partners? I'm not. You already know how to do all of those things, and at this stage when your desire is tiny and raw and blossoming, those things are the quickest way to kill it.

Instead, ask yourself *Who do I need to be in order to have it?* Do you need to be someone who can withstand the awkwardness of learning something "late?" Do you need to be someone who has enough confidence to venture to an unfamiliar faraway place? Or do you (ahem) need to be someone with the discipline to keep your butt in the chair and crank out a few hundred words every day?

Yes, the things you want require money, time, and discomfort. But before those will be of any use to you, they require the inner shift of becoming the kind of person who has or does that thing. If you skip the internal shifts, a tiny part of you won't ever feel ready and you'll find creative ways to sabotage yourself: You'll procrastinate, spend your money on other things that you tell yourself are vitally important but aren't, start a bunch of exciting but irrelevant new projects, or tell yourself you'll do it next month. You'll bury your desire, and in doing so, you'll bury what makes you feel alive.

For me to be the person I need to be in order to have my writing cottage, I need to be someone willing to take a stand for my writing, regardless of how the world defines success. I need to be someone who will invest in my own joy without demanding that it justifies itself with a book deal, a million fans, or a praiseworthy impact on the world. I need to be someone who holds the process of writing itself as sacred and valuable, deserving of its own temple.

So ask yourself, *Who do I need to become?* Sit with that question. Let it burn in your belly alongside your desire. Don't let the *Yeah But* Monster get you. Challenge yourself to make those internal shifts. And then watch as the path unfolds at your feet.

BEING *THAT* PERSON

Our family friend Alice makes a terrible house guest. She comes and goes as she pleases, stays out late, and no one ever knows whether to expect her for dinner. And this is just one part of the problem with Alice—the other being that in general no one can keep track of whether she's even in the country. When her husband died, she booked a trip to Zimbabwe where she stayed in a clay hut and told little kids stories about Jesus. She was in her 80s.

These are the problems that get rattled off when someone complains about Alice, but I know what the real problem is. That woman simply cannot be contained. She says what she thinks, goes where she wants, and sees no reason to negotiate her freedom with anyone, including the people who were hoping to treat her to their special pot roast recipe.

There's someone like Alice in every group. They refuse to go along with *the way we do things around here*—not because they want to cause trouble, but because they simply can't follow the unspoken rules. It would go against every part of who they are.

To be clear, I'm not talking about someone who gets off on being disruptive, hogging attention, and pissing people off. I'm talking about the person whose way of seeing things and doing things goes unapologetically against the grain–sometimes loudly, often quietly, always innocently. In families, this person is labeled the black sheep, the rebel, the troublemaker, the problem child. In any group, they become the scapegoat. All of the group's problems are seen as stemming from this lovely person who, as friendly as they are, simply can't just go with the flow. We'd all be so happy and peaceful if this one person would just get with the program.

Even if they're innocent in both intention and action, their disruption to the status quo is seen as willful disobedience. Worse yet, they don't even seem remorseful (because they're not). If you are this person—and believe me, you'll know if you are—please remember this:

You carry good medicine for any group. You have the gift of being able to see through the bullshit in a system, to see beyond *the way it's done.* You are able to understand things from all sides, from a bigger perspective. You've seen the invisible cages, and politely declined. And in doing so, you offer a unique vision for how things could evolve in a way that brings in more love, more peace, more joy, and more progress to everyone. Your medicine is very much needed.

But that doesn't always mean it's wanted. Disrupting the status quo, *the way we do things around here,* is not for the faint of heart. We humans hate change, even change that's good for us. We especially hate it if it wasn't our idea in the first place. When confronted with the horrible notion that there could be another, more fulfilling way of living life, our first reaction is to close our eyes, stick our fingers in our ears, and say *la la la la la* until it subsides enough that we can sidestep having to acknowledge it. We want to hide in the bushes until it passes.

But if that nagging threat of having to change our minds or our behavior doesn't pass quickly enough, our next reaction is to criticize it, mock it, or fight it. It becomes urgent to make it GO AWAY. It scares us because if we stop to consider it, we may have to loosen our death grip on what we are sure is the One Right Way. And that certainty we've been clinging to is the only thing keeping us sane in a world that feels out of our control. You better believe we're going to fight for it.

When you're someone who sees the bigger picture and questions the status quo, people are going to have strong reactions to your way of being. The greater their personal fear of not being in control, the harder they'll fight to shut you down, shut you up, and shut you out. When they do, it's excruciating.

So how do you hold this? How do you bring your precious, much-needed gifts to the world in a way that honors yourself and benefits everyone, without being burned alive?

You keep yourself intact by seeing peoples' reactions as what they are – a response to their own fear. Everyone has their limits on how far they can go past their comfort zone. And when their comfort zone is already being stretched against their will in a million other ways, their capacity to live and let live gets pretty damn small. Their scorn may be directed at you, but it's not personal. It's just easier to focus their irritation on you than it is to get to the bottom of what's really so unnerving about life itself.

The good news is, there are many other people like you. It's just a matter of doing what you do best: seeing beyond the obvious. Look for the other people who didn't make it into the Normal People Club. When you find each other, you'll enjoy a depth of friendship that is unparalleled. You may be pushed aside in one group, but on the perimeter is exactly where you'll find your soulmates. Instead of stopping the conversation, your way of being will light up the room.

TECHNICALLY SPEAKING

Any time the use of technology is up for discussion, you might as well cue the ominous music. Articles, podcasts, documentaries all warn of the dangers of too much screen-time. It wrecks focus, disrupts sleep, blocks connection, reduces empathy, and floods our brains with dopamine, turning us into spiral-eyed zombie squirrels. Experts every-where dole out the same prescription: create healthy limits.

In families with kids, this job is thrust on the grown ups: set arbitrary rules, elaborate earning systems, and app-con-trolled down time—and then consistently hold the line. We're expected to have daily battles against a palm-sized dopamine dispenser, placed in the hands of a young hacker who expertly maneuvers around every attempt to provide these so-called healthy limits. No one wins.

As adults, we're given all sorts of advice on how to create structure for ourselves. Buy this distraction-blocking app, create that routine, put your phone in another room and go back to using an analog alarm clock. Despite our best attempts, this rarely sticks. I put a one-hour daily limit on the browser on my phone and my mid-morning routine is to enter the passcode to bypass it. Yet I get to feel like I've done something admirable by setting it up in the first place.

So why not just relax and let life be one big screen-filled free-for-all? After all, we do a lot of productive, creative, connecting, and educational things on screens too, right? What's the real problem here?

I've heard the argument that teens and young adults need to put their phones down so someone can teach them basic life skills like how to change a tire, bake chicken breasts, or clean a toilet. The fear is that one day these budding adults will find themselves in a situation where they're stuck on the side of the road, negotiating cleaning duties with a roommate, or preparing to welcome their dinner date—and they'll be completely unequipped to handle it. They'll miss their job interview, disgust their roommate, or lose the person who could have been the one. They'll move back in with their parents due to lack of real world skills, and languish in the basement until they're 50. While I suppose this is a possibility, the other possibility is that they'll just find whatever they need on YouTube and get on with their life.

Missing an opportunity to learn how to do things is not the problem, especially since we can learn a lot of that online. The real challenge is maintaining a tolerance for things that don't involve an immediate hit of dopamine.

Let's back up for a second: What's the deal with dopamine? This feel-good neurotransmitter is released in the brain during activities that are highly rewarding or pleasurable. It brings feelings of pleasure, excitement, even euphoria. Dopamine is released when we eat something delicious, score the winning goal, or ace a test. In excess, it's blamed for addiction to substances or risky behaviors.

Our dopamine levels fluctuate depending on what we're doing. Slogging through your taxes is a much lower dopamine activity than seeing 23 new comments on your Instagram post or getting immersed in a tense Fortnite battle. Going on a picnic is low dopamine even if you're surrounded by your favorite people. Just the thought of something like that can make us twitchy. Like, you have to just sit around out there all afternoon? What if your phone dings? You just...*cringe*... ignore it?

Yes, that's exactly what you do. But we need to consciously develop a tolerance for going that long without the dopamine hit. Same applies for sitting through a drivers ed class, studying for an exam, or attending a half-day orientation for your new job. Even driving across town requires us to stop checking our notifications and pay attention to something boring like stop lights. These are the life skills we need in order to manage even the basics in our lives and they won't come from a quick YouTube tutorial. No one is going to teach us this—but if we're not careful, life itself will teach us in the form of failed classes, productivity struggles, and dissolving relationships.

If we don't consciously cultivate the tolerance for periods of low dopamine the default will be to fill every crack of time with a quick check here, a few videos there, just one short game while we wait for the next thing on the schedule. We automatically slip into the fog of the digital world where time passes unnoticed as we bask in a steady stream of that sweet, sweet chemical.

Arbitrary screen-time limits aren't the answer. However, being able to make decisions around what we want for our lives and then track ourselves both on and off screens is absolutely essential.

If you're going to play Fortnite for 12 hours a day, let that be an actual decision. But let it be a decision you make in the context of the bigger picture you have for your life. If you can get the degree you want while gaming until three in the morning, go for it! But don't just get on Fortnite until you feel like stopping and then look up at the clock, bleary eyed, scratch your head, tell yourself you'll start your essay tomorrow, shrug, and then do it again the next day.

As independent adults, the pressures of daily life forces a certain level of tracking. If we don't show up for our morning meeting because we were up late rabbitholing on YouTube the night before, our job is at risk...which means our ability to pay rent is in jeopardy, threatening the basic survival of ourselves and our families. We don't have the luxury of getting completely lost in tech.

When we're younger, the stakes aren't quite so high. You

might fail classes or have terrible hygiene, but at the end of the day you'll still have a roof over your head and someone will eventually make dinner. If you need to leave for school in five minutes, but you still haven't emerged from your room, chances are someone's going to come knocking and snap you out of it. And that makes it really hard to make smart choices. I mean, why should you? No wonder another five minute video wins over starting your math homework.

And that's at the heart of this battle in our families. Screen-time limits on their own are only effective if they're in support of something more important. And until we can define what that is it's just a setup for a frustrating dynamic.

Want a real screen-time plan? First think about what you want out of life. Maybe you want to get a college degree, learn how to play guitar, or make new friends. Even when these things require you to be online, it's in a lower dopamine way. You'll need to spend consistent blocks of time studying, practicing tedious chords, or picking your way through awkward initial conversations.

Next, decide how much low dopamine time you'll need to be able to tolerate in order to take the necessary steps to achieve those goals. Then make actual decisions around your screen-time. How much time should you spend unplugged in order to develop the ability to focus on low dopamine tasks like a two hour study block or a relaxed hangout with someone you're getting to know? And how much time will you have left over to indulge, enjoy, and just let loose on all of your favorite on-screen stuff?

Now your screen time limits actually serve a purpose: supporting you in getting what you want. Whether you do this through tracking apps, Wi-Fi controls, or a daily schedule, even longer days on screens can be considered healthy. And when you do get to indulge, you'll get a bigger bang for your dopamine buck. You'll get more satisfaction out of that time when it's free from the nagging feeling you really should be doing something else. Your limits are healthy not just because they're limits, but because they clear the time you need to create a life that will give you a natural rush of joy.

RADICAL RESPONSIBILITY

I was mid-travel when the initial COVID-19 upswing hit. A local friend and I had scheduled dinner together, excited to reconnect. As the night drew near we checked in with each other: *It's still cool to get together, right? We just have to be careful.* After weighing our options, we decided to meet at a restaurant with an outdoor patio. We showed up wearing face masks, sat at opposite ends of an eight-person table, and refrained from our usual goodbye hug, opting instead to wave politely from several feet away.

Three days later she texted to let me know that someone she had seen the weekend before was sick with the virus. Really sick, in fact. The next day, my friend tested positive.

I went on an anxiety fueled self disclosure spree. I called back home to give everyone heads up in case my kids would need to stay at their dad's house longer, which they probably wouldn't because after all, my friend and I had been so careful. I got tested right away, and dutifully answered daily texts saying, "No, still no results. They said it could be up to 10 days," along with reassurance that my friend and I had been the poster children for how to follow every precaution down to the letter so really there wasn't anything to worry about, but thanks for checking in.

And yet, people had opinions. My kids and their dad and stepmom urged me to quarantine in my hotel room for at least another week, aghast that I would even consider getting on a plane before I knew anything for sure. My boyfriend asked how come I was telling everyone and creating unnecessary anxiety when my test results were going to just come back negative anyway. A close friend questioned my decision to see anyone in person, period. I did a lot of agreeing with people, nodding in silent overwhelm, unable to speak up because everyone had a valid point and was simultaneously *missing* the point, which was that I was sincerely trying to do the right thing and keep everyone I love healthy.

One night it all got to be too much. I called my sweetest friend, overwhelmed from stuffing down my own emotional upheaval while absorbing the concern and judgment of everyone else. She shared a similar situation that was happening in her life, which she was desperately trying to manage responsibly as the whole thing went flying off the rails. "I'm racking up a lot of hate points," she laughed. "Me too," I replied. "But I think I have more," she pointed out, and she was right. She was definitely at the top of the leaderboard. Over the next week, that's how we'd check in with each other: "How are your hate points coming along?" It became our inside joke, our coded way of acknowledging the fact that trying to do the right thing is messy, unpredictable, and sometimes results in all sorts of upheaval. And we were going to be okay.

When things go sideways and blame starts getting thrown around, the most empowering thing you can do is to take radical responsibility. Radical responsibility is when you decide where to draw the line on what's actually your responsibility, and you go all in on taking care of the business that's yours. It allows you to act on those things with decisive precision and leave everything else where it belongs, with whom it belongs. Radical responsibility starts with getting clear on these questions:

1. What is my personal responsibility in this situation?
2. What is NOT my responsibility?
3. What is the responsibility of everyone else? Where do we share responsibility?

Once you're clear, then you're ready to turn this into a gift for yourself and others. Until then, tone it down, because all you'll bring is chaos.

Okay, you're thinking, great, so what if no one else is willing to take their share of the responsibility? Then it's perfectly acceptable to call them out, to tell them where you've just drawn the line on what's yours and what's theirs. Just know that even if you are very sweet, there is approximately 0.0001% chance that the other person will thoughtfully consider your point, nod, agree, and thank you for enlightening them. On the flip side, if you yell, insult, push, blame, and criticize, your message has *zero* chance of being absorbed. A message in that form raises defensive walls so fast that any receptivity you might have had is gone in an instant *even if what you have to say is true and would serve everyone.* The other person will try to quickly de-escalate the situation, thinking, "Wow, they're really losing it." It gives them an easy way out of having to listen to you because now the focus is on the drama of your delivery, not your message itself.

When I heard about my friend's test results, my responsibility was to get tested myself and to be honest and transparent with anyone who could be affected. Then I got to pass the responsibility baton. Now it was *everyone else's* responsibility to decide what to do with that information. If someone I had been in contact with wanted to go visit their elderly neighbor, it was up to them to weigh the perceived risk and make the judgment call. I might share my perspective if they asked, but it wasn't my job to talk them into or out of anything.

Even though I took radical responsibility I did not come out of that experience with any sort of badge of honor from the Responsibility Council. While my friend recovered quickly and my own test came back negative, my early transparency had caused fear in people I love, and what I thought would be straightforward and matter-of-fact conversations turned into angsty reactions and all sorts of opinions detailing the ways I had handled it wrong. I felt deeply alone, longing for someone to see me in my innocence, to acknowledge the way I took responsibility, and praise me for being both careful and honest. I felt like I handled the situation with integrity, but more than once I wished I hadn't told anyone anything. I wondered if quietly absorbing the stress all by myself would have been better than absorbing the stress of everyone around me.

I'm fortunate to have made it to the other side with negative test results and positive self esteem. Since I was clear on my responsibility and acted accordingly, I can let go of the judgements that came my way and move forward feeling satisfied that I acted according to my own values and stayed the course amidst the chaos.

When you step up and take radical responsibility and things *still* go sideways, just do your best, stay true to your inner compass, and trust that anything that gets shaken up or shaken loose could turn out to be exactly what's needed for everyone involved. You can't be attached to being praised, thanked, or validated. All you can do is tally up your hate points and go on boldly living, boldly loving.

TALK BACK TO ME
FOR EMBER

At a family gathering not long ago, the conversation with an older relative turned to a classic Boomer topic: Kids These Days. "Kids these days have no respect," they lamented. "They don't do as they're told. And have you heard the way they talk back?"

"Such a shame," I muttered, shaking my head and letting out a theatrical sigh. But if anyone had been paying close attention, they might have noticed the corners of my mouth turn up in a teeny tiny smirk.

When I was growing up, kids were expected to not talk back, which basically meant we couldn't openly disagree, question, or challenge anything we had just been told to do.

In those days, talking back could inflict any sort of punishment from being yelled at to being grounded, spanked, or having your mouth washed out with soap. If you talked back you were considered sassy, disrespectful, and disobedient—to both the irritated adult and to God, who had granted every adult on the planet the authority to tell you what to do. If a parent got a phone call from their kid's teacher, that kid was automatically guilty as charged. Their side of the story was irrelevant. They were just a kid.

During the first week of first grade, my friend Emma and I were showing each other the erasers we had just bought from the school office. We laid them out in neat little rows on her desk, the big pink rectangular ones, and little blue ones you stick on the end of a pencil. The bell rang and I grabbed my erasers and ran to my seat. Later that evening my parents got a phone call from Emma's parents. I had stolen some of Emma's erasers, they said, and we needed to get things straightened out. *Stolen?* I thought? No, I had grabbed my own erasers, but left hers. I tried to explain to my parents, but the charge stood.

Emma and her parents came to our house to sort things out. *I didn't steal anything*, I insisted, and now I was in trouble for lying, too. Emma sat quietly, looking at the floor. I was told to give her *all* of the erasers and to apologize to everyone in the room for lying and for stealing. I didn't want to hand over the erasers. They were the ones I had bought, after all, and...well, I was pretty sure I only took mine, but now with four adults staring me down I began to doubt. How could I be sure? They all looked alike. How many had I started with?

Emma glanced at me helplessly, just as trapped as I was in

this courtroom drama. The silence pressed against me from all sides. Everyone was waiting. I handed Emma my erasers and mumbled an apology for lying and stealing, which must have satisfied the adults because they all shook hands and Emma and her parents went home.

Emma's family moved away not long after that, and she and I didn't see each other again until college. "Remember that whole eraser thing?" she asked, rolling her eyes. "That was so ridiculous. I mean who knows what even happened. But they were five cent erasers, for Pete's sake."

Maybe the erasers were only five cents, but the emotional price was high. If I had continued to protest, I would have faced not only more shame, but punishment, too—because back then being a good parent meant holding the line no matter what. In my desperation to be seen as innocent and good, I wasn't willing to pay that price. So in order to escape the accusation of being a liar, I lied. In order to escape the charge of stealing erasers, I handed over my dignity.

That may be why I refuse to demand the same from you. And believe me, I've had, uh, "feedback" on my parenting from uncomfortable family members and friends. When one of you challenges me on something I've asked you to do, they would prefer that I escalate things. If you get loud, I should get louder. If you push back, I should push harder. They'd prefer I overpower your will until you shut up and comply. It's more comfortable for everyone that way.

But I won't. If you disagree with a decision I've made, I want you to speak up. I won't lie, when you do, it frustrates me to no end. I want to tear my hair out sometimes wondering why oh why does this dumb little thing have to be a battle? Couldn't you just suck it up and do it for heaven's sake so we can get out the door, get to bed, or get on with our lives? Everyone else is going along with the plan, so why do you have to act like this?

However, I choose not to overpower you with my because-I-said-so card unless it's absolutely necessary, and most of the time it's not. Instead, I get in the ring with you. You might dig in your heels, make snide comments, yell, cry, scream, and slam doors. I hold my ground and state my boundaries about what you or anyone else is allowed to say to me. If you cross the line into blaming, name calling, or saying mean things, I'll call you on it and coach you on a cleaner way to make your point. If it continues, I'll walk away. If you blame me, I'll point out where there's shared responsibility. You might disagree, and we might not solve it today or next week or until you're 35 and have your own kid carrying on about something. But I'll stick with the conversation even if we have to take breaks to cool down, and even if we have to keep coming back to it for days.

You won't always get your way, but I won't tell you you're a bad kid for feeling the way you do, and I won't forbid you from standing up for what you want. Because here's the thing: If you're never allowed to speak up, advocate for your position, and hold your ground, you start to lose access to the part of yourself that knows who you are, what you want, what you believe, and where your own boundaries are.

Let me be straight with you, though. There *is* a time and a place where the wisest thing to do is take a deep breath and zip your lips and go along with the program. Other times it's critical that you keep your composure while you take a stand. If you ever get pulled over by a cop, by all means advocate strongly and confidently for your legal rights, but now's not the time to lose your temper and start screaming insults to make your point. If you want to be effective, you absolutely MUST develop the skills and the judgment to deliver your point cleanly, with just the right amount of ferocity, at just the right time.

Some of the other "feedback" I've been "offered" is that I'm weak, ineffective, and unable to get a handle on my kids. But here's where I stand my own ground. Because the weak thing would be to overpower you until you shut up every time you challenge things in an inconvenient or uncomfortable way. It takes much more strength to be willing to stand my ground but hear you out, absorb your upset, and teach you how to advocate passionately for yourself in a way that allows you to actually be heard.

There's a nugget of truth in their criticism, though. Sometimes it might serve you better for me to force something. My commitment to helping you develop self-advocacy has in some ways cost me the upper hand. Not having the upper hand means I'm not always able to push you toward something I know is good for you. It's a tradeoff, and the people who love us are right to call me on it.

But I keep coming back to this: The world needs your way of thinking, your enormous capacity for empathy, and your passion for justice. By letting you "talk back" I'm letting you learn how to stay connected to those parts of yourself and give them a voice.

So don't sit down and don't shut up. Instead, learn how to express yourself skillfully. It's okay to be a little messy in the process. Explore those things here. I can take it.

MY MONEY, MY CHOICE
FOR AIDEN

When I was in college, any money I earned through my part-time job went toward what I could get *right now*: Ramen noodles in bulk, daily visits to the vending machine, and all-night hangouts at Perkins fueled by free refills on coffee. It also paid for a room in a drafty shared house and a horrible old car that spontaneously burst into flames in the backyard 6 months later. In my late 20s I celebrated the launch of my copywriting career by taking out a loan for a brand new car and spending all my remaining money on a hip apartment in downtown Seattle and fancy cocktails in fancy bars with my fancy friends.

In my 30s, you two came along and completely changed what I wanted out of my money. Forget trying to be hip or doing anything even remotely fancy. Now I wanted something that wasn't for sale: time.

Even though I had just invested a year and a half (and several thousand dollars) plugging away at massage school on nights and weekends, and even though massage felt like my soul's calling, I quickly began to resent my new career. Every time I signed up for a massage shift at the day spa, I had to pay someone to take care of you. Sometimes my shift would book up and I'd come home with a few hundred dollars in my pocket. But on slow days, I wouldn't even break even. I'd be stuck folding laundry in the breakroom while paying someone else to do what I longed to be doing—spending time with you.

I quickly retreated back to freelance writing, frantically cramming in assignments while you napped or answering emails at the kitchen counter, swaying back and forth while you sat at my feet and Ember fussed in the front carrier. I liked massage more than copywriting, but I loved you more than anything in the world. Money took on the sole purpose of giving me the choice of how to spend my time.

Now in my 40s I'm looking ahead to the next phase of my life. In 5 years you'll both be out of high school and on to college. (You're going to college, right? RIGHT? Seriously, don't make me write you another book.) I'm fortunate enough to be able to cover the bills, and fully aware of the privilege I carry that allows me to face an entirely different choice: how to invest in future long-term opportunities. Everything is up for re-evaluation. *Where would I like to live? How am I going to buy a home? Do I want to stick with the same career or do something entirely different?*

When I feel the impulse to buy something I think, "What do

I want more, another pair of shoes or a home in the southwest with a writing cottage out back?" When you know what your priorities are, the way you spend and save your money becomes a no brainer.

You'll be old enough next year to have your first real job. You don't currently need money for survival, which means everything you do with your money now is based on choice. The habits and mindsets you create now determine the foundation you'll have when you actually DO need money for survival—and beyond. Here are three things to remember as you head into adulthood:

Become an automatic saver. Don't rely on yourself to dutifully transfer money into a savings account on a regular basis. We lowly humans generally lack this kind of discipline. You'll tell yourself sweet little lies such as, *I'll start doing that when I get a raise* and *This month I have some unusual expenses, but next month I'll totally be back on track.* Or despite your best intentions, you'll procrastinate when your paycheck comes in until whoops, you spent it all, oh well, better luck next month.

The only way to succeed at this is to make it automatic. That means you set up a system that bypasses your moment-to-moment (unreliable) decision making process. Set up an automatic transfer from your checking to your savings account each month, or bypass your checking account altogether and have a portion of your paycheck deposited straight into your savings account. Aim for 10-30% of your income, if you can swing it. But even a small amount over time will add up—it's more about the habit than the percentage. Then leave your savings alone. Make it a one-way street, not a revolving door of money in and out. If you really suck at this like I do, set up your savings account in an entirely different bank and don't get a debit card linked to that account. Make it a huge pain in the butt to access that money so you can't transfer it on a whim while you're at Best Buy standing in front of a 75" TV that just happens to be on sale.

Protect your credit score. Based on what I've seen watching you on the Xbox, you're already a pro at going for points and boosting your score. I hate to ruin your fun, but I'd like to introduce you to a *new* point system: your credit score. There is no leaderboard, and it won't earn you upgraded weapons or cool skins or whatever. Instead, your credit score will earn you the ability to rent your own apartment and buy a reliable car. That's right, landlords won't rent to someone with a low credit score, and car dealerships won't let you do a payment plan unless you have the numbers to prove that you're unlikely to screw them over. Same goes for opening a credit card. And to buy your own home? Your credit needs to be *solid*. The higher your credit score, the lower the interest rate you'll get, which could save you tens of thousands of dollars over the course of a standard 30-year mortgage.

To be clear, having good credit does not mean *using* the credit available. Ideally you have credit you don't use or that you use lightly and pay off each month. Credit card companies love to prey on college students, setting up festive tables on campus and luring you into a high interest credit card by offering a $100 Amazon gift card if you sign up. Soon you're using your credit card for a meal here and a hoodie there, and before you know it you've racked up $1,000 in high-interest charges. Congratulations, you just got a $100 gift card and it only cost you $1,000 plus interest.

I won't go into all the details about building credit. There's a ton of information on the good ol' internet from people way more qualified than I am. But I want you to start getting strategic about this as soon as you turn 18, because your credit score is really a measure of your opportunities. It's basically the difference between driving a crappy car and paying me to live in my basement (please no) vs. driving a car you like to and from your own place, where you and your friends can blissfully play Xbox well into the night, finally free from annoying screen time limits and requests to pick up your dirty socks.

Always have your own bank account. Even if you're in a committed relationship and have a joint account for household expenses, always, *always* have a separate bank account that's just for you. I know, that's not very romantic. You know what else isn't romantic? Texting your partner from aisle 11 at Target to see if it's cool to buy a new vacuum cleaner and then wandering aimlessly for another 20 minutes until their meeting ends and they finally text you back to say go ahead. Or meticulously sticking to your teeny tiny grocery budget and then they home with a birdhouse, an ice cream maker, three new houseplants, and a bottle of $40 shampoo.

Having separate personal accounts is not only a good way to keep the peace, it's also a safety net. If anything goes wrong, you'll each have the money you need to take your next step, even if that next step means that you're moving forward on your own.

I have sooooo many regrets about my late 20s. Since I was finally earning more than I needed for basic survival, I should have been investing the few hundred extra dollars in a retirement fund instead of investing in the local bar scene. Since money still represented what I could get *right now*, and what I could get right now was another $15 cosmopolitan, my money went out as soon as it came in. I didn't have the perspective that building good habits now would give me an enormous return in freedom later.

As you start earning money, get clear on what it means to you and how you want to make it work on behalf of your values and goals. Then build your credit, start saving, and stay personally in charge of how you spend. That way you'll have what money truly represents: the freedom of choice for many years to come.

SOME LIKE IT HOT

While things like career, health, and friendships contribute to your overall wellbeing, nothing has the power to lift you up or slam you to the ground like a romantic relationship.

The good news is that it's not just luck that leads to a great relationship. The bad news is also that it's not just luck. It's discernment and ongoing work. Just like how learning to play the piano doesn't magically turn you into a virtuo-so violin player, personal development does not magically translate into good relationships. You can't meditate your way into listening skills. And no yoga workshop is going to teach you how to repair after a fight.

That said, all the couples' retreats and relationship articles in the world won't save you if you're forging ahead with the wrong person. So what traits should you look for when you're dating?

Here's what my list looked like in my 20s:

Hot
Exciting
Has a job

In my 30s, it grew to:

Decent looking
Exciting but not too exciting
Has a *good* job
Needs me in some way
Preferably no roommates

Now in my 40s, I've moved from a list of wishes to actual criteria—and an embarrassing percentage of them are on this list because I came limping out of one relationship or another vowing, "I'll never do THAT again!"

Of course, I still need to be attracted to someone and they must be a decent human being who is generally kind to me and others, etc. etc. But there's so much more than that. The nuances are really what make it or break it.

Here are my criteria now, along with my wishes that this will spare you needless heartbreak and give you a shortcut to a joyful relationship:

Able to regulate their own emotions. And "leaning on someone else all the time" must not be the way they do it. They must have something they do *on their own* to keep themselves grounded—something that does not require you to constantly absorb, fix, or sympathize in order to be supportive. I don't care what the thing is as long as it's healthy: meditation, working out, going for a drive, taking a long hike, building birdhouses, whatever. They'll still lean on you but it will be in a way that brings you closer, not pulls you under.

If they can't take care of themselves, you'll never be able to do enough to take care of them. You'll feel constant pressure to brush your own needs aside to be there for them, and eventually this lopsidedness will drain the life out of you and the relationship. You want a partner, not a project, and this means that you both rock your own self care.

No active addictions. It's impossible to have a healthy relationship with an addict. No matter how much they declare that they love you and need you, whatever they're addicted to will always be #1, and you'll always be #2. If their version of "emotional regulation" involves alcohol, drugs, sex, or overspending, don't get involved.

Good financial habits. Notice I didn't say "financially stable," and here's why: life has its ups and downs, and habits are more important that whatever the situation is in this moment in time.

I once dated someone who was making more than twice my income working for a hotshot investment firm. "Cool," I thought. "He's financially stable." I blissfully ignored red flags about his spending, trusting that everything was within his budget. A year later he filed for bankruptcy. It turns out he had managed to keep up the appearance of wealth while he slowly, invisibly went under. As his illusion shattered, so did his mental state. And predictably, our relationship tanked.

I'm writing this during the COVID-19 pandemic, when so many people are taking a financial hit even though they've done everything "right" financially. The man I love has created three solid income streams as a musician. He's respected in his industry, has a strong network, and has diligently saved and invested for years. He even found a way to teach online when most others in his industry could not. And yet with live music events being cancelled left and right, his income is in a temporary dip. Do I feel worried? Not one bit. His approach to money means he'll catch up when his industry picks up, or he'll find another income stream if it takes too long to recover. I'd much rather be with someone methodical who's going through a temporary dip than with someone who's making loads of money that evaporates the second it comes in.

Their time and their heart are available. I once heard a dating coach say that on the first date you should ask about their availability on two levels: practical and emotional. How much time do they have for a relationship? If they're working 60 hours a week, marathon training every Saturday, and spending every Sunday in ultimate frisbee tournaments, your relationship is only going to go so far. And how open do they feel toward intimacy? If they're nursing their wounds from a fresh breakup and still secretly pining for the one who got away, they won't be able to go all in on your relationship. It might seem okay at first but you won't feel like you have their heart, and that gets old fast. If you just want light, fun dating, that's fine. But if you want to create a deeper relationship, make sure they're willing to make you a priority in their calendar and in their heart.

They fight fair. I used to think that the measure of a good relationship was lack of conflict. I don't ever remember seeing my own parents fight. But a few years ago a friend of mine was in a couple's counselling session with her husband, as they halfheartedly tried to save their 12-year marriage. They weren't there to solve a particular issue, it's just that things felt kind of uninspired and distant. They had no burning desire to continue. It was all just *UGH*. Both of them had been trying to take the high road and keep the peace, while they each drifted off into their own separate orbits. The counselor looked at them sharply and said, "You know what you two need? You need a good fight! If you would just fight, that would be progress."

The key word here is a "good" fight. There's nothing wrong with being frustrated or outright angry with your partner, but you gotta express it in a way that's productive, not damaging. Damaging would be blaming the other person, name calling, making it all their fault, attacking their judgement, attacking their character, criticizing their values, talking down to them, giving them the cold shoulder, or scolding them in a way intended to shame them into better behavior.

A good fight would be describing what you're experiencing, telling them where your boundary is, and making a clear request for what you want instead. You don't have to be calm, but you do have to be clean. Are you standing against them or are you standing up for a higher vision of your relationship? A good fight is standing up for the relationship and advocating for what you need in order to keep showing up fully with an open heart.

Personally, I'd rather have someone yell and scream about how pissed off they are than to have someone look me in the eye and quietly tell me that I'm selfish and irresponsible and that our problems are all my fault. I can deal with displays of anger (as long as I don't physically feel in danger), but I can't deal with being on the receiving end of finger pointing and contempt, no matter how calmly it's delivered.

When your partner calls you out on something or presses you to change, ask yourself this: Am I being asked to diminish myself to accommodate some sort of dysfunction or am I being called to growth that makes our relationship stronger? Is the change required of me something that would make me shrink or would it bring out an even better version of myself?

If you need to fight, then by all means, please fight. But know what you're fighting for, so that the resolution is something that helps you grow and moves you forward together into even deeper intimacy.

They view relationships as an opportunity for personal growth. How willing is this person to learn, grow, and change in a relationship? Are they looking toward what they can learn or do they assume they have it all figured out by this point and "you get what you get"?

You'll learn a lot about someone's approach to relationships by listening closely to how they talk about their past relationships. Is everything their crazy ex's fault? Same with the ex before that and every ex before that one, from the beginning of time? And if they do acknowledge shared responsibility, how specific are they? Do they shrug and mutter something vague like, "Well, it takes two to tango, I guess," or can they name specific behaviors of theirs that contributed to the relationship strain? For example, "I wasn't willing to hear him out on his point of view without getting defensive, interrupting, and arguing. Pretty soon he stopped sharing things with me, and then he basically just shut down. When he cheated on me, that was a deal breaker for me and I ended things. But before that there was also a lot of hurt that had accumulated from the way we communicated, which basically eroded our relationship to the breaking point."

Growth requires reflection and honesty. Look for those traits and you'll know whether you have a future with this person.

They respect your creative gifts and won't compromise theirs. I've spent many relationships as a closeted writer. I quickly learned that to be open about my writing would put it under siege. Either the other person would demand to read everything I wrote or they'd make condescending comments about my "hobby." And then there's the crowd favorite, "I feel like your writing will always come first."

(Which it will, but please don't back me into that corner.) One person read my journal while I was at work, and that violation caused an irreparable wound. My writing is how I process life. Over and over I've written my way back out of the dark and lonely abyss. It's sacred. And it needs to be respected as such.

It's also a tremendous gift to be by the side of someone who's dedicated to their own creativity—to watch them glow as they describe what they're working on or to see the wide open joy on their face on stage. You are seeing a part of them that's only accessible through that form of expression. What an honor. Respecting their gift is respecting their soul. It's never a competition for love. It's an invitation into even more of it.

So, there you have it. These criteria may seem waaaaay too picky. Well, good. You're worth it. Come back next week and I'll have even more criteria for you. These are the things that make the joy of being in a relationship greater than the joy of being on your own. And isn't that what it's all about?

WITH FRIENDS LIKE THESE

While your choice in who you date has the power to make your life heaven or hell, your choice in friends paves the road to either destination.

We all need friends who are fun, free, and spontaneous. But the ones that last are the ones built on values you share and a mutual respect of each other's vulnerability and humanity.

Some friends sparkle, some friends glow. You'll find friendships that have an immediate sparkle. These people are exciting, daring, and full of creative, edgy ideas. You'll also find friendships that glow, meaning, they start off as warm and connected but in a quieter way. You connect over a common ground—a mutual friend, a shared interest, a class project—and gradually get to know each other better. These friends don't command attention, but there's something about them you sense you can trust. Over time your bond grows and they turn into someone you know you can count on, no matter what.

It's easy to become mesmerized by the sparkly people, following them like the Pied Piper into every adventure or entanglement. And that can be fun. But be sure to nurture your friendships that glow, because those are the ones that stay steady like a heartbeat, that you can come back to again and again.

Red flags in friendships

Just like there are red flags in dating, there are red flags to watch out for in a budding friendship. They're pretty much the same ones, but they somehow seem less alarming in a friendship so we're more likely to ignore them.

I'd like to introduce myself and my childhood trauma. Some people you meet share too much, too fast. Beware: this is a quick way to find yourself entangled in a role of supporter, which starts off feeling like a valiant hero and ends with feeling shackled in a prison of obligation. Maybe they endured terrible trauma earlier in life and it breaks your heart to know that something so unthinkable has happened to this beautiful human. So you stay close. You want to make them feel better, help give them a healing experience, prove to them that not all love is painful. Maybe they've considered ending their life, so now you feel like you need to be available to them day and night because what if... Early on it feels good to be the solid rock in their lives, and it feels reeeealllly good to be appreciated as their savior. But every savior gets crucified. As you attempt to unplug, reset, and get your own breathing room to stay grounded, their gratitude and appreciation quickly turns to panic, then pleading, then venom. They'll get passive aggressive and pouty, throw a tantrum, tell you that their pain is your fault, and accuse you of not caring.

Don't take the bait. People who reveal trauma very quickly tend to be sinking in their own quicksand. Be kind and supportive, but don't accept the role of supporter. If you do, you're joining them in that pit, and soon you'll find yourself in over your head, too. The most loving and supportive thing you can do is to offer to help them find resources, and then wish good things for them in their journey while you put your energy and attention on yours. If they can't handle that, it's time to firmly close the door.

You're fun until you're not. Does this person say they'll call but then they don't? Are they warm and friendly one day, cool and distant the next? Do they surprise you by inviting a bunch of their other friends along to the movie you thought you'd just be seeing with them? Does everything seem to revolve about them and their impulses, er, I mean, "spontaneity"? These friends are exciting, but they're not your glow friends. Take them for what they are — sparkly fun when you can get it. Don't try to be their sidekick, because as soon as you're not available or express the slightest hesitation about their shenanigans, they'll quickly replace you with someone who will happily and unquestioningly co-star in the show they're directing.

I helped you, so you owe me. At the tail end of a horrible breakup during my freshman year of college, I made a new friend. She was so sweet. She sat with me while I cried, listened while I processed my anger, and called me daily to see how I was doing. I appreciated her presence but felt a growing sense of unease as I got my feet back on the ground. Now she wanted to come over all the time, but I was ready for some space. I didn't want to talk about the breakup anymore, because I was focused on moving forward and enjoying life. I started savoring my solitude and needing to connect with my other friends, while this particular person was making herself at home in my dorm room, my text threads, and my voicemail. I felt smothered and found myself wanting to evade her frequent visits, but...now she was going through a breakup. She had been there for me, and what kind of a jerk just takes that support and disappears? So I smiled and played along, thinking that after I let her lean on me a bit we'd be about even, and THEN I'd start holding some boundaries.

But that internal sense of having repaid the emotional debt never came. And my lack of enthusiasm about the friendship was impossible to hide. I started taking longer and longer to return calls, being "in the middle of study group" when she was on campus, and ultimately sabotaging the friendship by being a friendly flake.

It's important to note that she herself never implied that I owed her. This was all me and my made up emotional accounting system. That's what made it such a tricky tangle to get out of. It's so easy to attach a sense of indebtedness to what should simply be gratitude. Sometimes the other person implies it or demands it. But the worst is when we do it to ourselves. We continue to override our internal boundaries. Since our gratitude lasts forever, so does our sense of owing that person our friendship—no matter how terrible they're acting. So we continue to override our own boundaries and dutifully give them our time and attention. This serves no one. Better to express your full, deep gratitude in a sincere card or phone call and then evaluate your relationship separately than to subconsciously feel the need to prove your gratitude through a halfhearted, ongoing friendship.

Being a good friend

What about those wonderful glow friendships? How do you keep and nurture and those? Like anything else, it comes down to learning a few skills.

Shut up and listen. Let's get the hardest one out of the way first. Learn how to listen without fixing, rescuing, playing devil's advocate, challenging their position, giving unsolicited advice, or trying to relate by jumping in with our own story. Most of us can't manage this because we get hijacked by our own reactivity. Our best intentions to listen last about 10 seconds and then the impulse to jump in takes over our brains and we blurt something out that stops their sharing in its tracks.

Learning to listen is really learning to stay present and regulate ourselves when we feel the impulse to react. No wonder we fail at this so much. It takes practice and discipline that starts with noticing what thoughts pop into your head while your friend is talking. Practice noticing that you have a thought and then quickly allowing it to pass, like sitting on the side of a road watching cars zoom by without chasing any of them down the road.

One way to make this easier is to decide you're going to be curious. In your mind, you're switching from the normal you with all of your opinions and helpful advice to a neutral observer, a scientist studying another species, curious about what makes this person tick. Try the "3 questions" method. When they tell you something, ask a question. When they answer, follow with another question that leads them deeper into the topic. And then a third. Once you're three questions deep, you'll not only learn something new, you'll be giving them the gift of feeling truly seen. The cool thing about this is that acting curious sparks actual curiosity. You'll leave the conversation more invigorated, too.

If, at the end, you're still dying to share your opinions, advice, or stories, just ask permission. "I have a thought that came up while you were talking. Are you open to hearing it?" Sometimes they'll say "no" and then thank goodness you didn't just climb onto your soapbox while they sat there feeling defeated and checked out. Sometimes they'll say yes, and then you have a receptive opening to a lovely conversation. I love it when someone asks my permission to share their advice because it allows me to notice where I am. Am I still so fired up about something that I don't want someone else's opinion? Do I still need to sort out my own thoughts before I can have a discussion about it? Or am I on the other side of those strong emotions and feeling open to other perspectives? Most of the time if someone asks (which they rarely do, by the way) my honest answer is "I do want your opinion and your advice, but I need to be upset a little while longer before I can hear it."

Do what you say you'll do. One of the things I appreciate most about my friend Leah is that when we make plans, I know she'll follow through. I don't have to wonder when she's going to cancel or check in with her the morning of to make sure we're still on. Seems like a no-brainer, but I've noticed a general social trend toward flakiness under the guise of self care. Feeling tired? Cancel your movie date. After all, you have to take care of yourself! Overloaded at work? Skip your dinner plans. It's important to not add more stress! Meanwhile, the person you just cancelled on feels obligated to set aside their disappointment and say something supportive and approving about your choice. You know what? Screw that. If you've reserved someone's time, show up for it. If you took on too much and now you regret having plans, follow through with your plans anyway and manage your time differently next time. Better to show up tired and keep it short and sweet than to be that person who can't be trusted to follow through. Trust is earned, and when you have it, honor it with your actions.

Tell them how much you appreciate them. Several months ago, my boyfriend and I started the daily practice of texting each other something we're grateful for in our relationship. This has infused our relationship with a spirit of positivity and mutual respect. We're choosing to see the good. It's also helped me become more comfortable expressing gratitude to my friends. I'm so often grateful for them, and now it occurs to me to actually say so.

Appreciate your sparkle friends and cherish your glow friends in both your words and your actions. Be a good friend by listening well, showing consistency, and earning and keeping trust. And always remember that a little gratitude goes a long way.

SORRY, NOT SORRY

We love telling little kids to say "I'm sorry" when they hit another kid, take their toy, or hurt their feelings. Those are the magic words that signal to everyone that it's time to get over it. It's quick and convenient. That's why when we hear someone squawking, we parents glance up from our phones and sigh, "Say you're sorry." Or as Ember so aptly put it the other day, "You mean you want me to manipulate the other person into liking me by telling them what they want to hear?"

Well, yeah, that's kind of what I had in mind. Plus, it's the quickest way to get the other kid's parents to stop giving us that judgy look because, see? I made my kid apologize. So there, Susan.

However, as we get older and make more damaging mistakes, "I'm sorry" just doesn't cut it. It might seem like the quickest way to get yourself off the hook while making the other person feel obligated to stop acting mad at you. What a relief, right? But at best, it stops the bleeding by rushing the process and setting the expectation that everyone brush everything under the rug and move on like nothing ever happened. It does nothing to make the other person feel like you've taken the time to reflect or empathize, and it doesn't build trust that it won't happen again—in fact, the other person can rightly assume that it will.

To make matters worse, most apologies are straight up lame. "I'm sorry, but..." is not an apology. It's an excuse couched as an apology. "That wasn't my intention" is also an excuse. It's very noble that you did not intend to hurt someone, but guess what? You did. Intention doesn't erase impact. And you're responsible for the impact.

Saying you're sorry is really more about you. It lets you move on at the other person's expense. It saves the moment but damages the relationship. On the other hand, an actual *repair* requires you to stop in the moment for the sake of helping the other person feel better. You're sacrificing your own comfort and antsiness to move on in order to regain their trust and deepen your relationship. It helps you move forward together.

How to do a proper repair

Acknowledge what you did, in detail. "When I was out with my friends, I ignored the time and kept you waiting an hour past when I said I'd pick you up to go to the movie. I didn't communicate with you and left you sitting there alone, unable to get a hold of me."

Take ownership of how you got there. "I was excited to reconnect with my old friends and I think a part of me just wanted to lose myself in the moment and stay out as long as everyone else did, without watching the clock. But I was afraid to disappoint you, so I committed to a movie with you at the time you suggested."

Acknowledge the impact it had on them. "You set aside a Friday night to hang out with me. You chose a movie, got all ready to go, and then just ended up sitting there waiting. That must have been a huge letdown and made you feel like I don't value your time or the fact that you made me a priority tonight." Ask them for feedback. "Is that right? Is there more? What else?" Then listen. Bite your tongue until it bleeds, but for the love of all things holy do NOT respond with explanations, excuses, or defenses. Listen, nod, and keep your mouth shut.

Say what you're going to do right now to make it right. "I know I can't rewind and do it over, but why don't you relax while I buy us tickets to the next show. My treat."

Commit to what you'll do differently in the future. "Next time I'll either book things on separate nights, or I'll set an alarm on my phone so I can be in the moment with those friends and still keep my commitment to you."

Ask if there's anything else they need from you. "Is there anything else I can do to help make it better? Then repeat the "keep your mouth shut" instructions in step 3.

Say "I'm sorry." The only reason I'm including this step is that those two words are so ingrained in our culture that the other person might not truly relax until they hear them. If you've done steps 1–6, you've already done your job. Add these two words to help their brain check that box and relax.

Let go of the results. Even if you've done an impeccable attempt at repair, the other person isn't obligated to open up and let you back in. Do what you can and then step back and give the other person space to do what feels right for them, on their own timeline. You've opened the door, and it's up to them whether they want to walk through it.

I've been on the receiving end of both apologies and repairs. Sometimes I can fully forgive and forget after an apology, but that's usually because I take it upon myself to do the work needed to release it. That should have been shared work, but I've had to do it on my own for the sake of my own peace. During a thoughtful repair, the emotional load on me is lifted. I've come out of the experience with an even deeper respect and appreciation for that person.

Repair is a radical act of compassion. To master the art of repair you need to master the art of setting aside your ego and dropping your defenses. This is black belt emotional ninja warrior stuff, to deprioritize your own experience for the sake of your relationship when every part of you desperately wants to explain your side of the story and be seen as the good person you are.

But here's where the true alchemy happens: After the dust has settled and the hurts have healed, you probably won't even feel the need to go back and explain. Your side vs. their side evaporates. Turns out repair works both ways.

YOUR EXPERIENCE MATTERS

So much of what I've offered here is about how to get where you want to go, have healthy relationships, rock your finances, and live an amazing life.

But living an amazing life isn't just about the outcome of your career, finances, or relationships. It's about the way you navigate the journey, and the gratitude you cultivate along the way.

Here in Seattle, everyone wants the bragging rights of having hiked Mt. Si. I've hiked it twice, and even though there's a great view at the top, I find the hike to be boooooooring. I mean, I ruined my knees on a death march up and down unrelenting switchbacks for 20 minutes of a view? What a lousy tradeoff. I'd much rather hike Mt. Teneriffe, which is more than 3 times the length and has a higher summit, but graces you with stunning wildflowers, dense forests, and breathtaking overlooks along the way. The summit itself is glorious, but even without the summit, the journey itself is worth it.

By all means, set your sights on the goals you want to accomplish and the person you want to be. Take radical responsibility, date wisely, manage your money, and show up to your friendships open hearted and fierce. But don't take your eyes off the journey itself. Pace yourself, look around, and take in all the messy brilliance along the way. The mountaintop is beautiful, but that's not where you unearth your own resilience. It's not where your gifts emerge. It's a nice resting place before you continue along your way, one step after the next.

THANK YOU

The list of people who have taught me about life—either accidentally or on purpose—would be its own book.

But Aiden and Ember, you are my greatest teachers. Your thoughtfulness, sensitivity, fiery passion for justice, and flat out refusal to be inauthentic means that I have constant work to do. Being a good parent to you requires a thousand deaths and a thousand resurrections. It's not for the faint of heart, so my heart grows strong. You hold my feet to the fire, and I discover that I can withstand the burn. It's alchemy of the best kind. I love you, always.

Love,
Mom

CPSIA information can be obtained
at www.ICGtesting.com
Printed in the USA
BVHW042222101021
618658BV00015B/740